TABLE OF CONTENTS

INTENTION

THE INTENTION FOR THIS MANUEL IS TO PROVIDE A COMPLETELY COMPREHENSIBLE ANALYSIS OF WHAT ASTROLOGY/ASTRONOMY IS IN ESSENCE, AND WHY IT IS IMPORTANT FOR AN INDIVIDUAL TO BECOME FAMILIAR WITH THEIR OWN NATO CHARTS.

EACH NATO CHART PROVIDES OUR SOULS BLUEPRINT FOR THIS LIFE, ONES STRENGTHS, WEAKNESSES, AND THE THEME IN WHICH WE INDIVIDUALLY PERCEIVE OURSELVES, REALITIES AND LIFE LESSONS. THIS CLOSELY RELATES TO OUR INDIVIDUAL ASPECTS, PERSONALITY TRAITS, AND CONNECTIONS WITH SELF AND OTHERS. PROVIDING US INSIGHT TO THE CAUSE OF WHY WE ARE THE WAY WE ARE.

WHAT IS SIDEREAL ASTROLOGY?

DEREAL ASTROLOGY REFERS TO ANY SYSTEM OF
STROLOGY THAT CALCULATES THE POSITIONS OF
ELESTIAL BODIES, RELATIVE TO THE ACTUAL
OCATION OF THE CONSTELLATIONS IN THE SKY AT
HE TIME OF AN INDIVIDUAL'S BIRTH.

NLIKE WESTERN ASTROLOGY, WHICH IS
ALCULATED BASED ON THE TROPICAL ZODIAC
YSTEM. THIS SYSTEM IS RELATED TO EARTH'S
EASONS AND THE POSITION OF THE SUN ALONG
HE ECLIPTIC (THE APPARENT PATH OF THE SUN
S IT MOVES TROUGH THE SKY OVER THE COURSE
F A YEAR). WESTERN CATERS TO A PERSPECTIVE
F ZODIAC GIVEN FROM EARTH RATHER THAN
VEN FROM THE STARS THEMSELVES.
HIS SYSTEM IS FIXED AND ALIGNS WITH THE
EASONS YEAR TO YEAR.

HIS TEXT RELAYS THAT SIDEREAL'S CALCULATIONS
OULD BE MORE ACCURATE, AS WESTERN
STROLOGY DOESN'T TAKE INTO CONSIDERATION
AT ALL THINGS INCLUDING PLANETS AND ORBITS
RE CONSTANTLY SHIFTING, AND EVOLVING.

E DIFFERENCES BETWEEN THESE TWO
ERSPECTIVES RESULT IN DIFFERENCES IN ZODIAC
ATES ASSOCIATED WITH EACH SIGN, ALONG WITH
FFERENT NATO CHART PLACEMENTS.

CONSTELLATION		SIDEREAL DATES
ARIES	♈	APR 15 - MAY 15
TAURUS	♉	MAY 16 - JUN 15
GEMINI	♊	JUN 16 - JUL 16
CANCER	♋	JUL 17 - AUG 16
LEO	♌	AUG 17 - SEP 16
VIRGO	♍	SEP 17 - OCT 17
LIBRA	♎	OCT 18 - NOV 16
SCORPIO	♏	NOV 17 - DEC 16
SAGITTARIUS	♐	DEC 17 - JAN 15
CAPRICORN	♑	JAN 16 - FEB 14
AQUARIUS	♒	FEB 15 - MAR 15
PISCES	♓	MAR 16 - APR 14

CONSTELLATION		WESTERN DATES
ARIES	♈	MAR 21 - APR 19
TAURUS	♉	APR 20 - MAY 20
GEMINI	♊	MAY 21 - JUN 21
CANCER	♋	JUN 22 - JUL 22
LEO	♌	JUL 23 - AUG 23
VIRGO	♍	AUG 24- SEP 22
LIBRA	♎	SEP 23 -OCT 23
SCORPIO	♏	OCT 24 - NOV 22
SAGITTARIUS	♐	NOV 23 - DEC 22
CAPRICORN	♑	DEC 23 - JAN 20
AQUARIUS	♒	JAN 21 - FEB 18
PISCES	♓	FEB 19 - MAR 20

1 INTRODUCTION TO THE SIGNS

In astrology, the Zodiac signs refer to the symbolic representation and manifestation of specific energy signatures, which inflicts influence on themes, personality traits, relationships, and life events of an individual.

REVIEWING THE ZODIAC WHEEL

THE VISUAL PLAY:

THE INTENTION OF THIS PLAY IS TO HELP FAMILIARIZE YOU WITH THE ENERGIES AND CHARACTERISTICS OF EACH SIGN, AS WELL AS THEIR ORDER WITHIN THE ZODIAC WHEEL.

ARIES

- THE FIRST OF THE SIGNS.
- THE SPARK, INITIATOR AND ASSERTIVE FORCE.
- THE GLYPH IS THE RAM SYMBOLIZING THE SIMILARITY BETWEEN ARIES' AND THE RAMS' ABILITY TO TAKE EVERYTHING HEAD ON.
- THE RAM HEAD BEING IDENTICAL TO THE SHAPE OF THE WOMB ALSO SYMBOLIZES THE BIRTH OF SOMETHING NEW. THE START OF THE ZODIAC.

THE VISUAL PLAY:

IMAGINE A SPECIES HAD TO RELOCATE TO A NEW PLANET FOR WHATEVER REASON. ARIES WAS THE FIRST OF THE ZODIAC TO WALK THIS NEW PLANET AND MANIFEST THEIR SPECIFIC ENERGY SIGNATURE INTO THIS REALITY.

AS THE GOD OF WAR, THEY GOT OFF THEIR SHIPS READY FOR THE CHALLENGES THEY MAY BE FACED WITH. THEY CAME GUNS BLAZING READY TO ANNIHILATED ANY THREATS AGAINST THEM. WITH A COMPETITIVE NATURE AND CHALLENGING FORCE, THEY STORMED THE FRONT LINES HEAD ON READY TO INITIATE A NEW ERA OF LIFE.

REVIEWING THE ZODIAC WHEEL

TAURUS

- EMBODIMENT OF EARTH
- MASTERS OF THE PHYSICAL SENSES.
- TENACIOUS, STUBBORN AND SENSUAL.
- THE GLYPH IS THE BULL
- REPERSENTING THEIR STABILITY, CONSISTENTCY, RELIABILITY AND LOYALTY.

THE VISUAL PLAY:

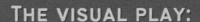

TAURUS GOT OFF THE SHIP IN AW OF THE BEAUTY'S OF THE NEW WORLD. THEY ARRIVED DETERMINED, READY TO STRIVE, IMMERSE AND INTEGRATE WITH THE ABUNDANCE OF THIS NEW LAND.

TAURUS IS FRUITFUL AND CONCURS THE ENVIRONMENT THEY WALK ON. THEY'RE COMMITTED TO BUILDING A COZY HOUSE, GROW DELICIOUS FOODS, LISTEN TO HARMONIOUS MUSIC, AND HAVE REPETITIVE DAYS THAT SUPPORT THE EXPERIENCES THEY WANT TO INDULGE IN.

THEY'RE HERE TO ENJOY AN OVERALL LIFE OF SENSUAL STIMULATION, PRIORITIZING FINANCIAL STABILITY AND AN IMPECCABLE WORK ETHIC, THAT WILL ALLOW FOR THINGS TO BE BUILT AND SUSTAINED THROUGH OUT THEIR ENDEAVOURS.

THEY CAME READY AND STEADY WORKING TOWARDS ACCUMULATING AN ABUNDANCE OF MATERIAL POSSESSIONS, WHILE SIMULTANEOUSLY BATHING IN THE BEAUTIFUL EXPERIENCES AND COMFORTABILITY THAT THEY CREATE FOR THEMSELVES THROUGH HARD WORK AND CONSISTENCY.

REVIEWING THE ZODIAC WHEEL

GEMINI ♊

- THE CHILD OF THE ZODIAC, THE CURIOUS MIND, THE COMMUNICATOR, THE TWINS, THE TRICKSTERS.
- QUICK WHITTED, AND MISCHIEVOUS.
- SYMBOLIZED BY THE TWINS TO REPRESENT THEIR DUAL PERSONALITY.
- THEY ARE THE PERSONIFICATION OF DUALITY.

THE VISUAL PLAY:

GEMINI GOT OFF THE SHIPS ASKING EVERY QUESTION THAT POPPED UP IN THEIR MINDS. WITH AN EAGERNESS TO LEARN, THEY ARRIVED POKING AND PRYING LOOKING TO SATISFY THEIR EVERY WONDER.

WITH A CURIOSITY LIKE NO OTHER, THEIR MINDS LEAD THEM TO DISCOVER NEW WONDERS OF THE WORLD THROUGH THE PATH OF QUESTIONING WHAT OTHERS MAY NOT.

THEY CAME READY TO SOCIALIZE, PARTICIPATE IN STRATEGIC GAMES, PLAYING TRICKS, AND INTELLECTUALLY CHALLENGING THOSE AROUND THEM ALONG THE WAY.

CANCER

- THE MOTHER OF THE ZODIAC, THE NURTURER AND CAREGIVER.
- THE INTUITIVE EMPATH
- SENSITIVE, EMOTIONAL DEPTH
- THE GLYPH IS THE CRAB; REPRESENTING THE HARD OUTSIDE AND SOFT INTERIOR. AS WELL AS THEIR PASSIVE NATURE BUT ABILITY TO PROTECT THEMSELVES IF PROVOKED.

THE VISUAL PLAY:

CANCER STEPPED OFF THE SHIPS WALKING SIDEWAYS, DIPPING ITS TOES IN THE WATER, TESTING IF THESE NEW WATERS WERE A SAFE AND SUITABLE PLACE FOR THEM TO CREATE A HOME.

THEY CAME READY AND WANTING TO NURTURE BOTH THEMSELVES AND THE OTHER SIGNS BY CREATING A SAFE SPACE OF EMOTIONAL VULNERABILITY AND COMFORT.

THEY TURNED FOOD INTO MEALS, AND HOUSES INTO HOMES. PROVIDING COMFORT AND ASSURITY AMONG THE COLLECTIVE. THEY INTRODUCED TRADITION AND CREATED ROOTS FOR A FAMILY ENVIRONMENT.

LEO

- THE SUN, THE SPOTLIGHT, THE SHOW.
- THE NATURAL BORN LEADER.
- CREATIVE, ROMANTIC, COMEDIC,
- YET COURAGEOUS, CONFIDENT , AND DRAMATIC, ALL AT ONCE.
- PRIDEFUL AND LOUD
- THE GLYPH IS THE LION, SYMBOLIC FOR LEO'S LOVE TO BASK IN THE SPOT LIGHT

THE VISUAL PLAY:

LEO WALKED OFF THE SHIP LIKE ITS THE RED CARPET. CHIN UP, CHEST OUT, DRESSED UP LIKE THE BEST OUT. THEY ANNOUNCED THEIR ARRIVAL TO ALL AND REPRESENTED THE EMBODIMENT OF SELF EXPRESSION IN THE MOST DRAMATIC WAYS. THEY WERE LOUD, FUNNY, CHARISMATIC AND CHARMING. THEY CAME HERE TO ENTERTAIN AND LEAD IN WAYS THAT ALIGN WITH THEM JUST BEING THEMSELVES.

REVIEWING THE ZODIAC WHEEL

VIRGO ♍

- THE THINKER, THE ANALYZER, THE ARCHITECT,
- THE AUTHOR. PERFECTIONIST AND CRITIC.
- SELFLESS, AND HELPFUL,
- SYMBOLIZED BY THE MAIDEN, REPRESENTING VIRGOS URGE TO SERVE THE COLLECTIVE AND THOSE AROUND THEM, UTILIZING THEIR MINDS AS THEIR GREATEST POWER.

THE VISUAL PLAY:

VIRGO WALKED OFF THE SHIP ADJUSTING THEIR GLASSES, SCANNING AND ANALYZING THE ENVIRONMENT AROUND THEM, WHILE TAKING NOTES ALONG THE WAY. PRIORITIZING THEIR VAST COLLECTION OF DATA AND INFORMATION TO MAKE DECISIONS AND FORM CONCLUSIONS.

THEY CREATED BLUEPRINTS OF ARCHITECTURAL DEVELOPMENTS TO BETTER STRUCTURE THE SYSTEMS IMPLEMENTED, TO BEST SERVE THE COLLECTIVE. SUCH AS; HEALTH SYSTEMS, PLANETARY IMPROVEMENTS AND SELFLESS ACTS OF SERVICE TO HELP THOSE IN NEED.

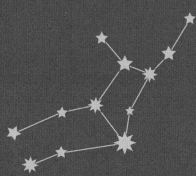

REVIEWING THE ZODIAC WHEEL

LIBRA ♎

- THE BALANCER, THE SOCIALITE AND DEVILS ADVOCATE,
- THE ADVISORS, MEDIATORS, AND CONSULTANTS.
- THE GLYPH IS THE SCALE TO REPRESENT BALANCE AND THE PERSONIFICATION OF INTEGRATING, LIGHT AND DARK, YIN AND YANG, IN ORDER TO SUSTAIN AN EQUILIBRIUM THROUGH OUT ALL ENDEAVOURS AND EXPERIENCES.

THE VISUAL PLAY:

LIBRA GOT OFF THE SHIP READY TO CONNECT, SUSTAIN RELATIONSHIPS AND SEEK HARMONY AND FAIRNESS IN ALL ASPECTS OF LIFE.

WITH CONSCIOUS SOLUTION BASED CONVERSATION, THEY SOUGHT OUT TO FIND THE SOLUTIONS TO EVERYONE'S PROBLEMS AND ESTABLISH MUTUAL UNDERSTANDINGS.

THEY ARE THE TRUE DIPLOMATS, PASSIVE DEFUSERS OF CONFRONTATION, AND GO TO'S FOR A NON BIAS WORD OF ADVICE. THEY BROUGHT FAIRNESS AND DIPLOMACY INTO THE WORLD.

SCORPIO ♏

- INTENSE, PASSIONATE, PROTECTIVE, AND MYSTERIOUS.
- OCCULTISTS AND INQUISITIVE MYSTICS
- THE INVESTIGATORS, PSYCHOLOGISTS.
- THE GLYPH IS THE THE SCORPION.
- SPITEFUL AND POISONOUS.
- REPRESENTED BY THEIR DESIRE TO REMAIN IN THE DARK AND UNSEEN SHADOWS OF THE WORLD.
- AS WELL AS THEIR ABILITY TO LEAVE AN UNFORGETTABLE STING IF PROVOKED.

THE VISUAL PLAY:

SCORPIO JUMPED OFF THE SHIP READY TO TEST ALL EXTREMES. MASTERS OF THE METAPHYSICAL SENSES. THEY WALKED THE PATH OF INTENSITY.

THEY DIVED INTO THE OCCULT TO UNCOVER ALL HIDDEN TRUTHS AND SOUGHT OUT THE DARK PLACES NO ONE ELSE DARED TO EXPLORE. THEY'RE REALM LEADERS OF THE TABOO, DEATH, SEX AND THE AFTERLIFE. SCORPIOS SECRETIVE NATURE AMPLIFIES THEIR MYSTERIOUS CHARACTERISTICS.

REVIEWING THE ZODIAC WHEEL

SAGITARIUS

- THE PHILOSOPHER
- THE POET
- THE MONK, AND EXPLORER.
- THE HERMIT
- FREE SPITED, BLUNT AND CLUMSY.
- THE GLYPH IS THE ARCHER, REPRESENTATIVE OF THEIR ABILITY TO HIT WHATEVER THEY'RE AIMING FOR.
- ALSO REPRESENTED BY THE CENTAUR FOR THEIR DESIRE FOR HIGHER KNOWLEDGE AND TRAVEL.

THE VISUAL PLAY:

SAGITTARIUS GOT OFF THE SHIP READY TO EXPERIENCE, TRAVEL AND EXPLORE. THEY PHILOSOPHIZED THEIR EXPERIENCES AND SHARED THEIR HIGHER KNOWLEDGE WITH THE COLLECTIVE.

THEY ARE THE SOLO WONDERERS AND ADVENTURERS, WITH A FIREY PASSION FOR FREEDOM, TRAVEL AND WISDOM THAT CANNOT BE CONTROLLED.

THEY LEARNED THROUGH EXPERIENCES RATHER THAN OBSERVATION AND SEARCHED FOR DEEPER MEANING WITHIN LIFE. WHILE CO EXISTING ALONGSIDE NATURE.

REVIEWING THE ZODIAC WHEEL

CAPRICORN ♑

- THE FATHER OF THE ZODIAC.
- PERSONIFICATION OF MASCULINITY.
- EXPERT ADDRESSORS.
- THE PROFESSIONALS, THE BUSINESS MAN.
- PERSISTENT, PATIENT & DISCIPLINED.
- THE SEA GOAT.
- REPRESENTING THEIR WILLINGNESS TO CLIMB THE HIGHEST MOUNTAINS TO REACH THEIR GOALS, AS WELL AS DIVE DEEP INTO WHATEVER THEY NEED TO BE SUCCESSFUL.

THE VISUAL PLAY:

CAPRICORN GOT OFF THE SHIP READY TO HANDLE BUSINESS. THEY LAID DOWN THE STRUCTURE FOR THE SIGNS TO TURN THEIR PASSIONS INTO CAREERS AND REPUTATIONS INTO LEGACY'S.

THEY ASSESSED EVERYONES STRENGTHS AND WEAKNESSES AND PUSHED THEM TOWARDS UTILIZING THEIR ABILITIES TO FORM A SUCCESSFUL ECONOMY. THEY ENFORCED TOUGH LOVE INTO THE ONES THAT NEEDED TO BE MOTIVATED IN ATTEMPT TO STRENGTHEN THE GROUP AS A WHOLE. THEY CREATED A REPUTABLE LEGACY BY PROVIDING FINANCIAL STATUS AND PROFESSIONAL DECORUM.

AQUARIUS ♒

- THE HUMANITARIAN
- THE VISIONARY
- UNIQUE, INDIVIDUALISTIC, AND INNOVATIVE,
- THE BLACK SHEEP
- BLUNT, DETACHED AND AUTHENTIC
- THE WATER BEARER; REPRESENTING THEIR ABILITY HOLD THE EMOTIONS OF THEMSELVES, AND THOSE AROUND THEM. THE ONE STRONG ENOUGH TO BEAR THE WEIGHT."WATER BEARER".

THE VISUAL PLAY:

AQUARIUS GOT OFF THE SHIP REVOLUTIONIZING THE WORLD AROUND THEM. THEY BROUGHT FORTH A NEW ERA OF INNOVATION BY IMPLEMENTING TECHNOLOGIES, THAT WOULD CHANGE HOW THE COLLECTIVE INTERACT WITH THE WORLD. THEY SPARKED EVOLUTION BY UNIQUELY PAVING THE PATH OF INDIVIDUALISM AND FOUGHT UNAPOLOGETICALLY AGAINST SYSTEMS THAT THREATENED THEIR IDEALISM.

PISCES ♓

- THE DREAMER
- MYSTICAL, MAGICAL AND ROMANTIC.
- COMPASSIONATE, IMAGINATIVE AND CREATIVE.
- THE ARTIST.
- PSYCHIC, EMPATHETIC, SENSITIVE, MOODY.
- THE GLYPH IS TWO SWIMMING FISH, REPRESENTING THEIR ABILITY TO REMAIN IN THE PHYSICAL AND THE DREAM REALM.

THE VISUAL PLAY:

PISCES GOT OFF THE SHIP FANTASIZING ABOUT THE MAGICAL POSSIBILITIES OF THE NEW WORLD. THEY CARRIED THE ABILITY TO CHANNEL THE FEELINGS OF ALL THINGS AROUND THEM, THE PLANET, ITS ANIMALS AND ALL ITS INHABITANTS. THEY BECAME THE BRIDGE BETWEEN THE DREAM REALM AND PHYSICAL REALITY, AND REFLECTED THAT THROUGH THEIR VARIOUS DIFFERENT ART FORMS AND ABILITIES.

POLAR/SISTER SIGNS

DEFINITION:

SISTER SIGNS ARE AN EMBODIMENT OF YIN AND YANG PRINCIPALS, ENFORCING BOTH LIGHT AND DARK, MASCULINE AND FEMININE PHYSICAL AND NON PHYSICAL ASPECTS OF EACH SIGNS. SISTER SIGNS ARE ACROSS FROM EACH OTHER IN THE ZODIAC WHEEL.

- "SISTER" AS IN RELATED, NOT ALWAYS RELATABLE. BUT ARE STILL BORN OF THE SAME "PARENTS", MEANING SOURCE (AXIS) OF ENERGY'S, YET AT OPPOSITE SIDES OF OF THE SPECTRUM.

- THE RELATIONSHIP BETWEEN SISTER SIGNS CAN BE SEEMINGLY SIMILAR YET INDEFINITELY DIFFERENT FROM ONE ANOTHER. THIS CAUSES CHALLENGING CONFLICTS BUT ALSO CREATING COMPLIMENTARY CHEMISTRY BETWEEN SIGNS

- ALL SISTER SIGN ARE COMPLIMENTARY ELEMENTS IN NATURE. FIRE PAIRED WITH AIR AND WATER WITH EARTH.

ARIES ♈
QUALITIES

SIMILARITIES

LIBRA ♎
QUALITIES

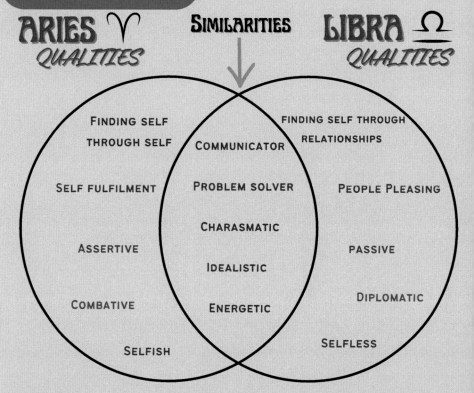

FINDING SELF THROUGH SELF

SELF FULFILMENT

ASSERTIVE

COMBATIVE

SELFISH

COMMUNICATOR

PROBLEM SOLVER

CHARASMATIC

IDEALISTIC

ENERGETIC

FINDING SELF THROUGH RELATIONSHIPS

PEOPLE PLEASING

PASSIVE

DIPLOMATIC

SELFLESS

COMMUNICATOR : ARIES HAS AN ASSERTIVE NATURE THAT MAKES THEM NATURALLY EXPRESSIVE, BOLD AND DIRECT, ESPECIALLY WHEN CHALLENGED. ON THE OTHER HAND LIBRA IS A KNOWN COMMUNICATOR AS THEY ARE SOCIAL INDIVIDUALS WHO ENJOY CONNECTING WITH OTHERS THROUGH CONVERSATION AND DIALOGUE.

PROBLEM SOLVER: ARIES ARE HIGHLY PROACTIVE AND APPROACH CHALLENGES WITH CONFIDENCE AND STRONG DETERMINATION. TAKING ISSUES HEAD ON. LIBRA IS VERY DIPLOMATIC AND APPROACHES CHALLENGES THROUGH WEIGHING ALL FACTORS. VALUING HARMONY AND BALANCE.

CHARISMA: ARIES IS CHARISMATIC THROUGH ITS DYNAMIC, AND CONFIDENT NATURE, WHILE LIBRA'S CHARM IS OFTEN EXPRESSED THROUGH ITS GRACIOUSNESS AND ABILITY TO MAKE PEOPLE FEEL COMFORTABLE.

ENERGETIC: ARIES IS ENERGETIC THROUGH THEIR COMPETITIVENESS, THE PASSION AND ENTHUSIASM THEY FEEL TOWARDS LIFE WHICH POWERS THEM. LIBRA IS ENERGETIC DUE TO THEIR OUTGOING AND SOCIABLE NATURE. THEY THRIVE ON INTERACTION AND COMMUNICATION WITH OTHERS.

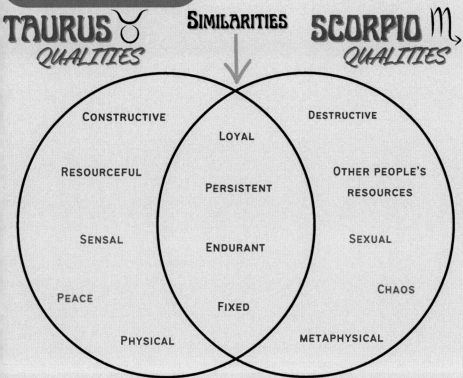

TAURUS ♉
QUALITIES

SIMILARITIES

SCORPIO ♏
QUALITIES

Taurus: Constructive, Resourceful, Sensal, Peace, Physical

Similarities: Loyal, Persistent, Endurant, Fixed

Scorpio: Destructive, Other people's resources, Sexual, Chaos, Metaphysical

LOYAL: Taurus values stability, security and dependability in relationships, thus making them loyal by nature. Scorpio creates profound emotional connections with others and carry an intense protectiveness for those they love.

PERSISTENT: Taurus demonstrates their persistence through their steady and methodical approach to tasks. Scorpio, however, has an intense determination that is fuelled by their deep emotions and passions, making them relentless in pursuit of what they desire.

ENDURANCE: Taurus is known to be a consistent and stubborn sign, giving them the ability to persevere through challenges without giving up easily. Scorpio are highly resilient and passionate, giving them the strength and energy to alchemize resistance.

FIXED: Both Taurus and Scorpio are fixed signs, meaning they are resistant to change, regarding how they express their energies. Taurus being stubborn, stable and persistent, they prefer to stick to consistent circumstances. Scorpio being intense, deep and protective, creates complexity for this sign, making it hard for them to see past the depth of their own emotions.

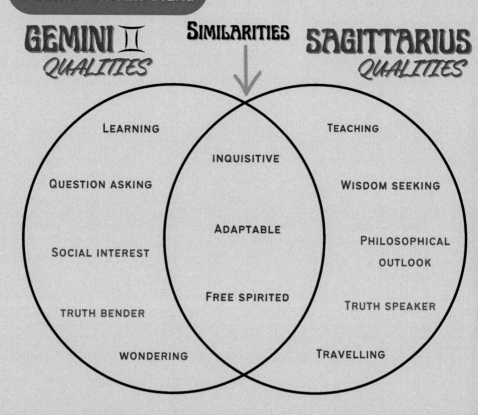

GEMINI Ⅱ
QUALITIES

SIMILARITIES

SAGITTARIUS
QUALITIES

LEARNING

TEACHING

INQUISITIVE

QUESTION ASKING

WISDOM SEEKING

ADAPTABLE

SOCIAL INTEREST

PHILOSOPHICAL OUTLOOK

FREE SPIRITED

TRUTH BENDER

TRUTH SPEAKER

WONDERING

TRAVELLING

INQUISITIVE: GEMINI HAS A DESIRE FOR LEARNING AND DISCOVERY, ASKING QUESTIONS TO ACQUIRE INFORMATION ON VARIOUS TOPICS, IDEAS AND PERSPECTIVES. SAGITTARIUS ARE DRAWN TO EXPLORING KNEW IDEAS, CULTURES AND PHILOSOPHIES TO EXPAND THEIR KNOWLEDGE OF THE WORLD AND ACQUIRE WISDOM.

ADAPTABLE: GEMINI EXPRESSES DUALITY IN THEIR PERSONALITY, ALLOWING THEM TO NAVIGATE DIFFERENT SOCIAL DYNAMICS AND EMBRACE CHANGE. SAGITTARIUS ARE VERY CURIOUS AND OPENED MINDED, GIVING THEM THE WILLINGNESS TO EXPLORE NEW EXPERIENCES.

FREE SPIRITED: GEMINI POSSESS A PLAYFUL AND YOUTHFUL ENERGY. THEIR PLAYFULNESS ALLOWS THEM TO FOSTER A SENSE OF SPONTANEITY, FLEXIBILITY AND OPENNESS TO NEW EXPERIENCES. SAGITTARIUS HAVE A STRONG DESIRE FOR EXPLORATION. WITH AN ADVENTUROUS NATURE AND LOVE OF TRAVEL, THEY ARE NATURAL RISK TAKERS, UNAFRAID TO VENTURE INTO THE UNKNOWN IN PURSUIT OF DREAMS AND ASPIRATIONS.

CANCER
QUALITIES

SIMILARITIES

CAPRICORN
QUALITIES

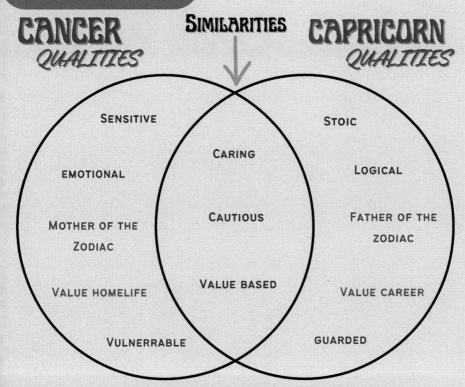

SENSITIVE

STOIC

CARING

EMOTIONAL

LOGICAL

MOTHER OF THE
ZODIAC

CAUTIOUS

FATHER OF THE
ZODIAC

VALUE BASED

VALUE HOMELIFE

VALUE CAREER

VULNERRABLE

GUARDED

ARING: CANCER HAS A NATURAL INCLINATION TOWARDS NURTURING AND AREGIVING. THROUGH OFFERING EMOTIONAL SUPPORT, COMFORT AND CREATING SAFE ENVIRONMENT. CAPRICORN OFTEN SHOW THEIR SUPPORT THROUGH RACTICAL ACTIONS RATHER THAN AFFECTION. THROUGH ESTABLISHING TABILITY, SECURITY AND COMMITMENT FOR THEMSELVES AND THE ONE THEY LOVE.

AUTIOUS: CANCERS ARE HIGHLY SENSITIVE AND INTUITIVE SIGNS, WHO APPROACH MOTIONAL SITUATIONS WITH CAUTION. WARY OF WHO THEY OPEN UP TO, REVEAL HEIR VULNERABILITIES TO, AS WELL AS PROTECTING THEIR FAMILY LIFE AND ERSONAL SPACES. CAPRICORN, HOWEVER, IS CAUTIOUS IN A MORE PRACTICAL ENSE. PRUDENT WITH THEIR FINANCES, REPUTATION AND BUSINESS ELATIONSHIPS.

ALUE BASED: CANCER NATURALLY EXPRESSES THE VALUE OF CULTIVATING EMININE ENERGY, ENCOURAGING THOSE AROUND THEM TO GAIN COMFORTABILITY ITH THEIR FEMININE ASPECTS OF EMOTIONAL VULNERABILITY. CAPRICORN, OWEVER, DEMONSTRATE THEIR VALUE BASE THROUGH THE USE OF MASCULINE NERGY. INFLUENCING DISCIPLINE, RESPONSIBILITY AND THE VALUE OF PRINCIPAL.

LEO
QUALITIES

SIMILARITIES

AQUARIUS
QUALITIES

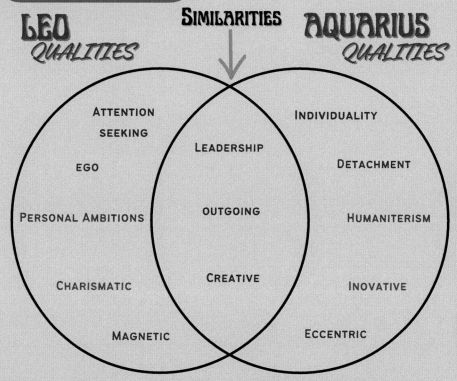

ATTENTION SEEKING

EGO

PERSONAL AMBITIONS

CHARISMATIC

MAGNETIC

LEADERSHIP

OUTGOING

CREATIVE

INDIVIDUALITY

DETACHMENT

HUMANITERISM

INOVATIVE

ECCENTRIC

LEADERSHIP: LEO HAS A MAGNETIC PRESENCE. CONFIDENT, CHARISMATIC AND PASSIONATE, THEY POSSES THE ABILITY TO INFLUENCE OTHERS BY ALLOWING THEM TO FEEL INSPIRED AND MOTIVATED. AQUARIUS HAS A VISIONARY PERSPECTIVE, ABLE TO SEE POSSIBILITIES OTHERS MAY OVERLOOK AND ARE NOT AFRAID TO THINK OUTSIDE THE BOX. INDEPENDENT AND HUMANITARIAN, THEY ARE DRIVEN BY SOCIAL RESPONSIBILITY, UNAFRAID TO GO AGAINST THE GRAIN.

OUTGOING: LEO IS EXPRESSIVE IN COMMUNICATION, COMFORTABLE SHARING THEIR THOUGHTS, FEELINGS AND IDEAS WITH OTHERS. THEIR CONFIDENCE OFTEN ATTRACTS SOCIAL MAGNETISM, AS THEY ARE NOT AFRAID TO PUT THEMSELVES OUT THERE. AQUARIUS IS OUTGOING IN INTELLECTUALLY STIMULATING DISCUSSIONS AND THEIR PURSUIT OF SOCIAL CHANGE.

CREATIVE: LEO IS CREATIVE THROUGH THEIR DRAMATIC EXPRESSION. THEY HAVE A THEATRICAL FLAIR THAT CAN BE VERY CAPTIVATING. THEIR CREATIVITY CAN BE PRONE TO BE EXPRESSED THROUGH VISUAL ARTS, MUSIC, PERFORMANCE OR SENSE OF STYLE. AQUARIUS HAS A REPUTATION FOR THEIR ORIGINALITY AND INNOVATION. OFTEN HAVING UNCONVENTIONAL IDEAS AND APPROACHES. ALSO POSSESSING A SENSE OF ECCENTRICITY AND INDIVIDUALITY.

VIRGO QUALITIES
SIMILARITIES
PISCES QUALITIES

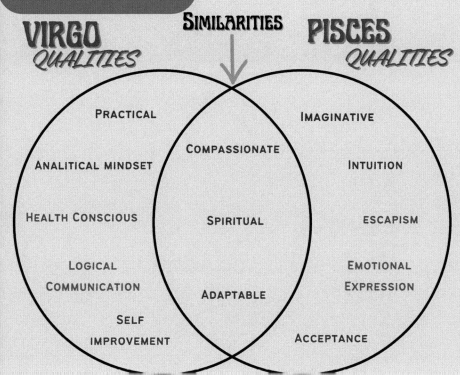

VIRGO
- PRACTICAL
- ANALITICAL MINDSET
- HEALTH CONSCIOUS
- LOGICAL COMMUNICATION
- SELF IMPROVEMENT

SIMILARITIES
- COMPASSIONATE
- SPIRITUAL
- ADAPTABLE

PISCES
- IMAGINATIVE
- INTUITION
- ESCAPISM
- EMOTIONAL EXPRESSION
- ACCEPTANCE

COMPASSIONATE: VIRGO IS OFTEN COMPASSIONATE BECAUSE THEY POSSESS A DEEP GENUINE DESIRE TO HELP OTHERS. THEIR ANALYTICAL NATURE ALLOWS THEM TO UNDERSTAND PEOPLE'S NEEDS AND SITUATIONS, LEADING THEM TO OFFER PRACTICAL ASSISTANCE AND SUPPORT. PISCES ARE COMPASSIONATE DUE TO THEIR DEEPLY EMPATHETIC AND SENSITIVE NATURE. THIS ALLOWING THEM TO CONNECT WITH PEOPLE ON A PROFOUND LEVEL.

SPIRITUAL: VIRGO POSSESS A DESIRE FOR SELF-IMPROVEMENT. THEIR INTROSPECTIVE NATURE MIGHT LEAD THEM TO SEEK SPIRITUALITY THROUGH PRACTICES SUCH AS MEDITATION, YOGA, OR MINDFULNESS, AS THESE PRACTICES ALIGN WITH THEIR NEED FOR STRUCTURE AND BALANCE IN THEIR LIVES. PISCES POSSES A NATURAL INCLINATION TOWARDS THE MYSTICAL AND THE UNSEEN REALMS. THEY ARE SENSITIVE TO THE ENERGIES AROUND AND MAY HAVE VIVID DREAMS, PREMONITIONS OR INTUITIVE INSIGHTS THAT GUIDE THEM ON THEIR SPIRITUAL PATHS.

ADAPTABLE: VIRGO APPROACHES TASKS UTILIZING THEIR ANALYTICAL MINDSET. THEIR WILLINGNESS TO LEARN AND IMPROVE, ALLOW THEM TO SEEK OUT NEW INFORMATION AND SKILLS THAT CAN HELP THEM NAVIGATE UNFAMILIAR SITUATIONS OR ENVIRONMENTS. PISCES IS CREATIVE AND IMAGINATIVE, ALLOWING THEM TO APPROACH CHALLENGES FROM MULTIPLE ANGLES AND THINK OUTSIDE THE BOX WHEN NECESSARY.

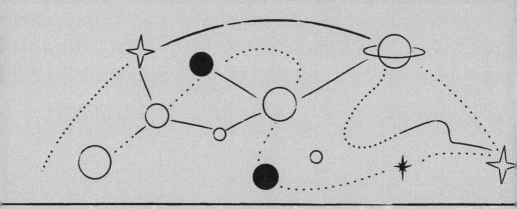

2 ASTROLOGY ANATOMY

ASTROLOGY ANATOMY REFERS THE FUNDAMENTAL COMPONENTS THAT MAKE UP THE SIGNS AND NATO CHART. THIS INCLUDES HOUSES, RULING PLANETS, ELEMENTS, AND MODES.

CHART BREAK DOWN

Each nato Chart is composed of 12 houses that are ruled by the 12 signs. each sign has planetary rulers that are 'home' in their sign's houses.

Example:

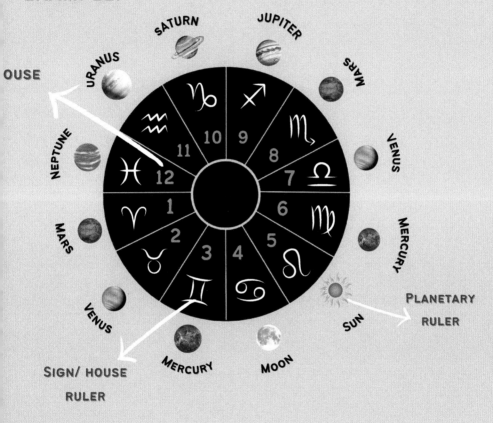

...OUSE

SATURN

JUPITER

URANUS

MARS

NEPTUNE

VENUS

MARS

MERCURY

VENUS

SUN

PLANETARY RULER

Sign/ house ruler

MERCURY

MOON

...EFINITIONS

...OUSE: A HOUSE IS AN AREA OF LIFE THAT CORRESPONDS TO SPECIFIC THEMES ...ND EXPERIENCES RELATING TO THE ATTRIBUTES OF THEIR HOUSE RULER/SIGNS.

...OUSE RULER: THE SIGN THAT RULES THE HOUSE

...LANETARY RULER; THE PLANET THAT RULES THE SIGN

ELEMENTS

MODES

The elements refer to four fundamental qualities associated with the twelve signs. They provide insight into the qualities and energies of each sign, influencing their behavior and approach to life.

The modes are the setting in which the elements are expressed through each sign. This categorizes the signs based on their approach to change and adaptation

FIRE

Passionate, Dynamic, Direct, Energetic, Spontaneous, Confident.

EARTH

Grounded, Materialistic, Stable, Consistent, practical

AIR

Intellectual, Communicative, social, Outgoing, Mental

WATER:

Intuitive, emotional, empathetic, Refletive

CARDINAL:

Cardinal signs are initiators. Known for their proactive an assertive approach to change They are often associated wit beginnings, innovation, and taking charge.

MUTABLE:

Mutable signs are adaptable, flexible, and versatile. skilli at navigating transitions and adjusting to new circumstances. associated wi changeability, versatility, an fluidity.

FIXED:

Fixed signs are resistant to change. Known for their commitment, persistence, and consistency.

SUN

Ruler of: Leo

CHART
SYMBOL:

(SIGN TYPE:)

FIRE, FIXED

THE SUN REPRESENTS THE CORE ESSENCE OF AN INDIVIDUAL'S PERSONALITY, VITALITY, AND EGOIC IDENTITY. IT GOVERNS YOUR UNCONSCIOUS EXPRESSION AND INTERESTS. THIS RESULTS IN EVERY COMPONENT IN THE NATO CHART REFLECTING YOUR SUN. PARALLEL TO HOW THE SUN HAS THIS EFFECT TO EVERYTHING ON OUR PLANET AND SOLAR SYSTEM.

I AM, I SHINE , I EMBODY

MOON

Ruler of: Cancer

(SIGN TYPE:)

WATER, CARDINAL

THE MOON REPRESENTS THE INNER SELF, EMOTIONS, AND INTERNAL OASIS. IT DEALS WITH OUR EMOTIONAL NEEDS, AND HOW WE NURTURE OURSELVES AND OTHERS. IT REFLECTS OUR INTUITIVE ABILITIES, RECEPTIVITY TO CHANGE, AND HOW WE PROCESS AND RESPOND TO OUR ENVIRONMENT ON AN EMOTIONAL LEVEL.

I FEEL, I'M DRAWN, I CARE

Chart Symbol:

☿

MERCURY

Ruler of: Gemini & Virgo

(Sign type:)
Air, Mutable

(Sign type:)
Earth, Mutable

Mercury represents how we process information and energy logically, and how we express ourselves through communication. It's role is to mentally conceptualize energy from planets, and move energy from planet to planet through thought. It is associated with communication, intellect, logic and adaptability. It rules over areas such as writing, speaking and decision making.

I THINK, I PROCESS, I SPEAK

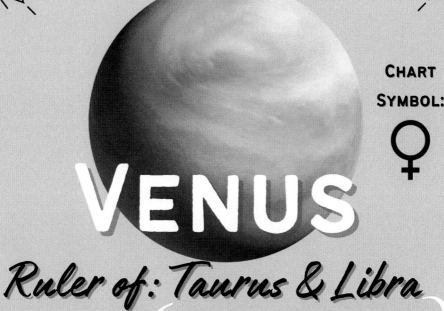

CHART SYMBOL:

♀

VENUS

Ruler of: Taurus & Libra

(SIGN TYPE:)
EARTH, FIXED

(SIGN TYPE:)
AIR, CARDINAL

VENUS REPRESENTS ONES LOVE LANGUAGE. THIS CONSIST OF WHAT EXPERIENCES AND QUALITIES THAT WE VALUE BOTH IN LIFE AND OTHER PEOPLE, AS WELL AS HOW WE EXPRESS OUR ADMIRATION AND AFFECTION TOWARDS THEM. VENUS IS THE PLANET LOVE IS MANIFESTED THROUGH. AND IS RESPONSIBLE FOR THE ENJOYMENT OF EXPERIENCES. THIS PLANET ALSO REPRESENTS THE ABUNDANCE OF MONEY AND THE LUXURIOUS THINGS IN LIFE.

I LOVE, I VALUE, I ATTRACT

MARS

CHART SYMBOL: ♂

Ruler of: Aries & Scorpio

(SIGN TYPE:) FIRE, CARDINAL | **(SIGN TYPE:)** WATER, FIXED

MARS REPRESENTS ENERGY, PASSION, DRIVE, ASSERTIVENESS, AND AGGRESSION. IT REPRESENTS OUR PHYSICAL ENERGY, COURAGE, DETERMINATION, AND HOW WE ASSERT OURSELVES IN THE WORLD. MARS ALSO GOVERNS OUR SEXUAL DESIRES AND HOW WE PURSUE OUR GOALS. IT'S PLACEMENT IN A BIRTH CHART CAN INDICATE HOW WE EXPRESS THESE TRAITS AND HOW WE HANDLE CONFLICT AND COMPETITION

I DO, I DESIRE, I ASSERT

CHART SYMBOL:

♄

SATURN

Ruler of: Capricorn

(SIGN TYPE:)

EARTH, CARDINAL

SATURN REPRESENTS DISCIPLINE, RESPONSIBILITY, STRUCTURE, RESTRICTIONS AND AUTHORITY. IT SYMBOLIZES AREAS OF LIFE WHERE WE ENCOUNTER CHALLENGES, WHERE WE NEED TO WORK HARD, AND WHERE WE CAN EXPERIENCE DELAYS OR OBSTACLES. REPRESENTING AREAS WE NEED TO DEVELOP PATIENCE AND PERSEVERANCE.

I PERSIST, I DISCIPLINE,

CHART SYMBOL:

2

JUPITER

Ruler of: Sagittarius

(SIGN TYPE:)

FIRE, MUABLE

JUPITER REPRESENTS EXPANSION, GROWTH, ABUNDANCE, OPTIMISM, AND LUCK. IT SYMBOLIZES OPPORTUNITIES, HIGHER LEARNING, AND WISDOM. JUPITER GOVERNS AREAS OF LIFE WHERE WE SEEK TO BROADEN OUR HORIZONS, TAKE RISKS, AND EXPLORE NEW POSSIBILITIES. IN THE CHART IT SHOWCASES WHERE WE ARE NATURALLY FORTUNATE AND EXPERIENCE ABUNDANCE.

I EXPAND, I EXPLORE, I GROW

CHART SYMBOL:

URANUS

Ruler of: Aquarius

(SIGN TYPE:)

AIR, FIXED

URANUS IN THE CHART REPRESENTS ORIGINALITY, REBELLION, INNOVATION, INDEPENDENCE AND CHANGE. IT GOVERNS AREAS OF LIFE WHERE WE EXPERIENCE UNPREDICTABILITY, AND THE DESIRE FOR FREEDOM FROM LIMITATIONS. IT RELATES TO TECHNOLOGY, PROGRESS AND SOCIAL REFORM. IN THE CHART IT REPRESENT WHERE WE SEEK TO BREAK FREE FROM STATUS QUO, EMBRACE INDIVIDUALITY, AND PURSUE OUR UNIQUE VISION FOR THE FUTURE.

I TRANSFORM, I CHANGE

CHART
SYMBOL:

NEPTUNE

Ruler of: Pisces

(SIGN TYPE:)

WATER, MUTABLE

NEPTUNE REPRESENTS, IMAGINATION, DREAMS, ILLUSION, SPIRITUALITY, AND THE SUBCONSCIOUS MIND. IN THE CHART IT INFLUENCES DEEPER EXPLORATION OF THE SPIRITUAL AND EMOTIONAL DIMENSIONS OF SELF. HOWEVER IT CAN ALSO CREATES ILLUSION, CONFUSION, AND ESCAPISM FOR AN INDIVIDUAL.

I DREAM, I IMAGINE,

CHART
SYMBOL

PLUTO

Co-Ruler of: Scorpio

(SIGN TYPE:)
WATER, FIXED

PLUTO REPRESENTS, TRANSFORMATION, DEPTH AND INTENSITY. IT'S PLACEMENT IN THE CHART INDICATES AREAS OF LIFE WHERE SIGNIFICANT CHANGES, UPHEAVALS AND REBIRTH MAY OCCUR. IT CAN BRING AWARENESS TO UNCONSCIOUS PATTERNS, MOTIVATIONS AND DESIRES. BUT ALSO HELP INDIVIDUALS SHED OLD PATTERNS, BELIEFS AND ATTACHMENTS TO UNDERGO PROFOUND INNER TRANSFORMATION.

I TRANSMUTE, I EMPOWER

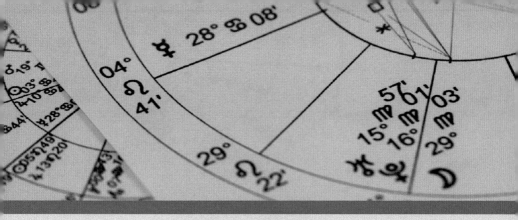

HOUSES

Definition:

A HOUSE IS AN AREA OF LIFE THAT CORRESPONDS TO SPECIFIC THEMES AND EXPERIENCES RELATING TO THE ATTRIBUTES OF THEIR HOUSE RULER/SIGNS.

1st house

House ruler: Aries

THE SIGN THAT GOVERNS THE HOUSE IS BASED ON THE ORDER OF THE ZODIAC. EI; ARIES IS THE FIRST ZODIAC SIGN, MEANING THE RULER OF THE 1ST HOUSE. ARIES IS RULED BY MARS ALSO MAKING MARS THE RULING PLANET OF THIS HOUSE

(*THE PLANET RULES THE SIGN, AND THE SIGN RULES THE HOUSE.*)

THIS HOUSE MANAGES THESE THEMES OF LIFE:

- SELF
- APPEARANCE
- BEGINNINGS
- THE BODY.
- FIRST IMPRESSIONS
- ATTITUDE
- IDENTITY,
- APPROACH TO LIFE

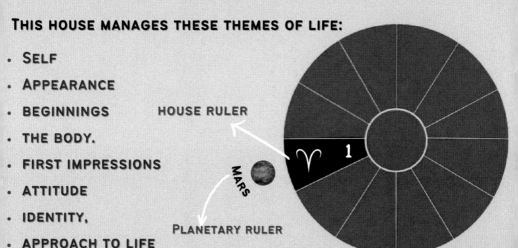

HOUSES

2nd house

House ruler: Taurus

Taurus is the second zodiac sign, meaning the ruler of th[e]
2nd house. Taurus is ruled by venus also making venus th[e]
ruling planet of this house

(*The planet rules the sign, and the sign rules the house.*)

This house manages
these themes of life:

- Money
- work
- income
- Daily routines
- Values
- material possessions
- priorities
- habits
- your job
- worth ethic

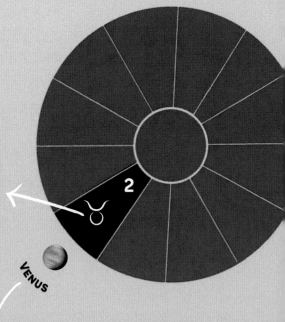

HOUSE
RULER

VENUS

Planetary
ruler

HOUSES

3RD HOUSE

HOUSE RULER: GEMINI

GEMINI IS THE THIRD ZODIAC SIGN, MEANING THE RULER OF THE 3RD HOUSE. GEMINI IS RULED BY MERCURY ALSO MAKING MERCURY THE RULING PLANET OF THIS HOUSE

(*THE PLANET RULES THE SIGN, AND THE SIGN RULES THE HOUSE.*)

THIS HOUSE MANAGES THESE THEMES OF LIFE:

- THE MIND
- COMMUNICATION
- SIBLINGS
- SOCIAL ACTIVITY
- NEIGHBOURS
- EARLY EDUCATION
- LOCAL EXPLORATION

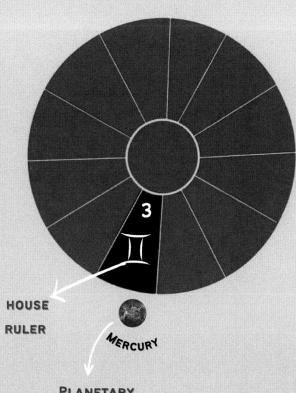

HOUSE RULER

MERCURY

PLANETARY RULER

HOUSES

4TH HOUSE

HOUSE RULER: CANCER

CANCER IS THE FORTH ZODIAC SIGN, MEANING THE RULER OF THE 4TH HOUSE. CANCER IS RULED BY THE MOON ALSO MAKING THE MOON THE RULING PLANET OF THIS HOUSE

(*THE PLANET RULES THE SIGN, AND THE SIGN RULES THE HOUSE.*)

THIS HOUSE MANAGES
THESE THEMES OF LIFE:

- HOME
- ROOTS
- FAMILY
- SELF CARE
- EMOTIONS
- FOUNDATION
- MOTHERHOOD
- CHILDREN
- WOMAN
- FEMININITY

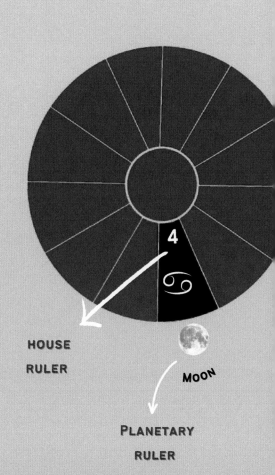

HOUSE
RULER

MOON

PLANETARY
RULER

HOUSES

5TH HOUSE

HOUSE RULER: LEO

LEO IS THE FIFTH ZODIAC SIGN, MEANING THE RULER OF THE 5TH HOUSE. LEO IS RULED BY THE SUN, ALSO MAKING THE SUN THE RULING PLANET OF THIS HOUSE

(*THE PLANET RULES THE SIGN, AND THE SIGN RULES THE HOUSE.*)

THIS HOUSE MANAGES
THESE THEMES OF LIFE:

- ROMANCE
- LOVE AFFAIRS
- PLAY
- CREATIVITY
- FERTILITY
- CHILDLIKE SPIRIT
- JOY
- SELF-EXPRESSION
- DRAMA

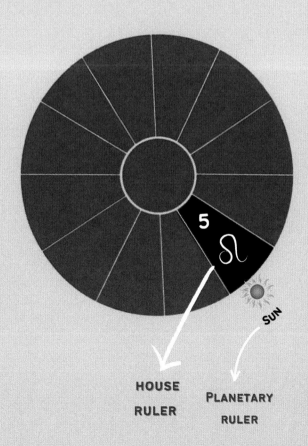

HOUSE
RULER

PLANETARY
RULER

HOUSES

6TH HOUSE

HOUSE RULER: VIRGO

VIRGO IS THE SIXTH ZODIAC SIGN, MEANING THE RULER OF THE 6T[H]
HOUSE. VIRGO IS RULED BY MERCURY, ALSO MAKING MERCURY TH[E]
RULING PLANET OF THIS HOUSE

(*THE PLANET RULES THE SIGN, AND THE SIGN RULES THE HOUSE.*)

**THIS HOUSE MANAGES
THESE THEMES OF LIFE:**

- ROMANCE
- LOVE AFFAIRS
- PLAY
- CREATIVITY
- FERTILITY
- CHILDLIKE SPIRIT
- JOY
- SELF-EXPRESSION
- DRAMA

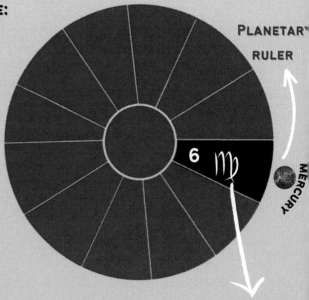

PLANETARY
RULER

MERCURY

6 ♍

HOUSE
RULER

HOUSES

7th House

House ruler: Libra

Libra is the seventh zodiac sign, meaning the ruler of the 7th house. Libra is ruled by Venus, also making Venus the ruling planet of this house

(*The planet rules the sign, and the sign rules the house.*)

This house manages these themes of life:

- Relationships
- marriage
- contracts
- business partners
- equality
- sharing
- interpersonal style

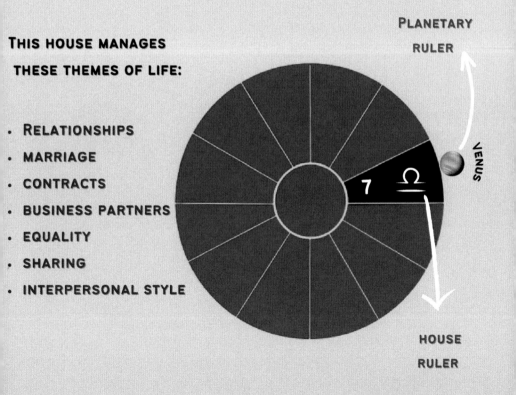

Planetary ruler

Venus

House ruler

HOUSES

8TH HOUSE

HOUSE RULER: SCORPIO

SCORPIO IS THE EIGHT ZODIAC SIGN, MEANING THE RULER OF THE 8TH HOUSE. SCORPIO IS RULED BY MARS, ALSO MAKING MARS THE RULING PLANET OF THIS HOUSE

(*THE PLANET RULES THE SIGN, AND THE SIGN RULES THE HOUSE.*)

THIS HOUSE MANAGES THESE THEMES OF LIFE:

- MERGING
- SEX
- THE OCCULT
- INTIMACY
- SHARED FINANCES
- INHERITANCES
- TAXES
- LOANS
- ASSESTS
- PROPERTY
- JOINT VENTURES
- GOALS
- MYSTERY
- PARTNER'S RESOURCES

PLANETAR RULER

MARS

HOUS RULE

8

HOUSES

9TH HOUSE

HOUSE RULER: SAGITTARIUS

SAGITTARIUS IS THE NINTH ZODIAC SIGN, MEANING THE RULER OF THE 9TH HOUSE. SAGITTARIUS IS RULED BY JUPITER, ALSO MAKING JUPITER THE RULING PLANET OF THIS HOUSE

(*THE PLANET RULES THE SIGN, AND THE SIGN RULES THE HOUSE.*)

THIS HOUSE MANAGES
THESE THEMES OF LIFE:

- TRAVEL
- WISDOM
- PHILOSOPHY
- HIGHER EDUCATION
- LAW & RELIGION
- CROSS-CULTURAL
- LEARNING
- ETHICS

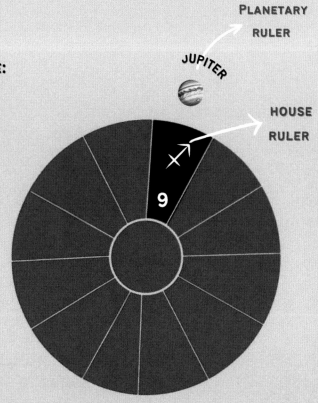

PLANETARY RULER

JUPITER

HOUSE RULER

HOUSES

10TH HOUSE

HOUSE RULER: CAPRICORN

CAPRICORN IS THE TENTH ZODIAC SIGN, MEANING THE RULER OF THE 10TH HOUSE. CAPRICORN IS RULED BY SATURN, ALSO MAKING SATURN THE RULING PLANET OF THIS HOUSE

(*THE PLANET RULES THE SIGN, AND THE SIGN RULES THE HOUSE.*)

THIS HOUSE MANAGES
THESE THEMES OF LIFE:

- CAREER
- LONG-TERM GOALS
- STRUCTURE STATUS
- REPUTATION
- PUBLIC IMAGE
- MASCULINITY
- MEN
- FATHERHOOD
- EXPERTS
- FAME & RECOGNITION

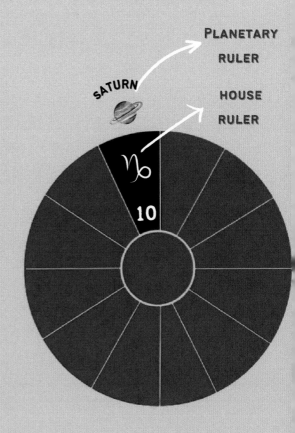

PLANETARY RULER

HOUSE RULER

SATURN

HOUSES

11th house

House ruler: Aquarius

Aquarius is the eleventh zodiac sign, meaning the ruler of the 11th house. Aquarius is ruled by Uranus, also making Uranus the ruling planet of this house

(*The planet rules the sign, and the sign rules the house.*)

This house manages these themes of life:

- Groups
- Friends
- Social awareness
- Humanitarianism
- Technology
- Hopes and wishes
- The future

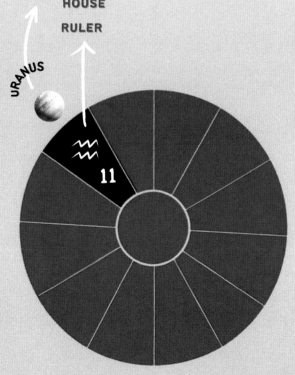

Planetary ruler

House ruler

Uranus

11

HOUSES

12TH HOUSE

HOUSE RULER: PISCES

PISCES IS THE TWELFTH ZODIAC SIGN, MEANING THE RULER OF TH
12TH HOUSE. PISCES IS RULED BY NEPTUNE, ALSO MAKING
NEPTUNE THE RULING PLANET OF THIS HOUSE

(*THE PLANET RULES THE SIGN, AND THE SIGN RULES THE HOUSE.*)

THIS HOUSE MANAGES
THESE THEMES OF LIFE:

- ENDINGS
- HEALING
- CLOSURE
- SPIRITUALITY
- SOLITUDE
- KARMA
- OLD AGE
- AFTERLIFE
- WHAT'S HIDDEN
- LIMITING BELIEFS
- SUBCONSCIOUS

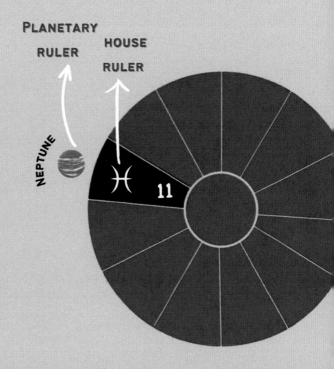

3 CELESIAL POINTS

IN ASTROLOGY, CELESTIAL POINTS REFER TO THE SPECIFIC POSITIONS OF CELESTIAL BODIES IN THE NATAL CHART. SUCH AS PLANETS, ASTEROIDS AND THEIR PLACEMENTS. PROVIDING MORE LAYERS OF INTERPRETATION AND INSIGHT.

ASCENDANT (RISING SIGN)

Big 3: The Ascendant, also known as the rising sign, is part of what we call , the "Big 3", alongside the moon and the Sun sign. these 3 signs represent the core aspects of self and play a crucial role in shaping a person's character, personality and life path.

The rising sign is used to determine an individual's outer personality, demeanour, and first impressions that a person makes on other's. It reflects how individual's represent themselves to the world and the mask they wear in social interactions.

 ## Location:

The Ascendant in a birth-chart, will usually be located in the first house. Typically represented by a line that extends the horizon point, and is usually labeled "AC" or "ASC", followed by the zodiac sign the house is in.

DESCENDANT

The Descendant is associated with relationships, partnerships, and how you relate to others, especially in one-on-one interactions. It reflects the qualities you seek in a partner and the type of relationships you're drawn to. Additionally, it can indicate how you project yourself onto others and the qualities you attract or encounter in close relationships.

 ## Location/Symbol

The Descendant is opposite to the Ascendant in the natal chart, and is usually located on the cusp of, or in, the 7th house. It will usually be abbreviated as "Dsc".

CHIRON

Chiron is considered a minor asteroid, which is often referred to as the "Wounded healer". Chiron is associated with themes of healing, transformation, and the integration of wounds or perceived weaknesses into strengths. It represents the area of life where we may experience deep emotional or psychological wounds, as well as our potential for healing and growth through facing and working with these wounds.

 ### Location:

Chiron's placement in the chart can vary, as it moves through the zodiac like other celestial bodies.
It has an assigned symbol to identify where it is placed in the chart, and determine what energy and area of life it is manifested through

Chiron symbol in the natal birth chart:

NORTH NODE

NORTH NODE IS ONE OF THE LUNAR NODES, IT REPRESENTS THE FUTURE, GROWTH, AND THE PATH ONE IS MEANT TO FOLLOW IN THIS LIFETIME. IT'S SEEN AS A POINT OF DESTINY, INDICATING CHALLENGES AND LESSONS THAT NEED TO BE LEARNED FOR PERSONAL DEVELOPMENT AND FULFILMENT. IT'S PLACEMENT IN A NATAL CHART SIGNIFIES THE QUALITIES AND EXPERIENCES THAT AN INDIVIDUAL SHOULD STRIVE TO EMBRACE AND INTEGRATE INTO THEIR LIFE TO FULFILL THEIR SOUL'S PURPOSE

 ## LOCATION/SYMBOL

IN A NATAL CHART, THE NORTH NODE IS REPRESENTED BY A SYMBOL THAT LOOKS LIKE AN UPSIDE-DOWN HORSESHOE. ITS PLACEMENT IS INDICATED BY THE ZODIAC SIGN AND HOUSE IT OCCUPIES.

SOUTH NODE

South node is the opposite point to the north node. It represents past experiences, intergraded habits, traits and behaviours carried over from previous lifetimes or earlier in current life. It's associated with comfort zones, familiar patterns, and reliant tendencies. It provides insight within the natal chart as to the areas where an individual may need to release in order to grow and evolve. Normally demonstrating where you're coming from in this life, and the path towards the north node would make where you're walking towards in evolution.

 ### Location/Symbol

In a natal chart, the south Node is represented by a symbol that looks like a horseshoe, or a "u" shape. Its placement is indicated by the zodiac sign and house it occupies.

MIDHEAVEN

THE MIDHEAVEN , ALSO KNOWN AS THE "MEDIUM COELI (MC)" REPRESENTS THE HIGHEST POINT IN THE SKY AT THE TIME OF YOUR BIRTH. IT IS ASSOCIATED WITH ONE'S PUBLIC IMAGE, CAREER, GOALS, AMBITIONS, AND REPUTATION. IT SIGNIFIES HOW YOU ARE PERCEIVED BY THE WORLD AT LARGE AND YOUR ASPIRATIONS IN TERMS OF CAREER AND ACHIEVEMENTS. THIS PLACEMENT OFFERS INSIGHTS INTO THE TYPE OF CAREER PATH OR PUBLIC ROLE THAT MAY BE FULFILLING FOR YOU.

 ## LOCATION/SYMBOL

IN A NATAL CHART, THE MIDHEAVEN (MC) IS TYPICALLY LOCATED AT THE TOP OF THE CHART, IN OR ON THE CUSP OF THE 10TH HOUSE. IT'S ONE OF THE FOUR MAJOR ANGLES IN THE CHART, THE MIDHEAVEN IS TYPICALLY REPRESENTED BY A VERTICAL LINE THAT INTERSECTS WITH THE HORIZONTAL LINE.

BLACKMOON LILTH

In astrology, Black Moon Lilith is a hypothetical point in space that represents a specific aspect of the dark feminine archetype, Black Moon Lilith is not a physical celestial body but a calculated point based on the lunar apogee, which is the point in the moon's orbit farthest from earth.

Black moon Lilth is often associated with themes of rebellion, independence, sexuality, shadow aspects, primal instincts, and the repressed or marginalized aspects of the feminine. It can signify areas where one may experience feelings of rage, taboo, or empowerment, as well as where one may face societal or personal challenges related to asserting their autonomy or confronting suppressed emotions.

 ### Location/Symbol

In a natal chart, Black Moon Lilith is often represented by a crescent moon with a small cross beneath it.

VERTEX

N ASTROLOGY, THE VERTEX IS A POINT THAT REPRESENTS SIGNIFICANT CONNECTIONS AND FATED ENCOUNTERS IN A PERSON'S LIFE. IT IS NOT A CELESTIAL BODY LIKE A PLANET OR A STAR, BUT RATHER A CALCULATED POINT BASED ON THE INTERSECTION OF THE PRIME VERTICAL.

THE VERTEX IS ASSOCIATED WITH ENCOUNTERS, RELATIONSHIPS, AND EVENTS THAT FEEL DESTINED OR FATED. IT'S OFTEN INTERPRETED AS A POINT OF KARMIC CONNECTION, INDICATING MEETINGS OR EXPERIENCES THAT HAVE A PROFOUND IMPACT ON THE INDIVIDUAL'S LIFE PATH. SOME ALSO INTERPRET THE VERTEX AS A POINT OF SPIRITUAL AWAKENING OR SOULMATE CONNECTIONS.

 ## LOCATION/SYMBOL

IN A NATAL CHART, VERTEX IS REPRESENTED BY EITHER THE WORD VERTEX, OR IS ABBREVIATED AS "Vx".

PART OF FORTUNE

In astrology, the Part of Fortune is a calculated point that represents a person's potential for success, happiness, and fulfillment in life. It's not a celestial body but is determined based on the positions of the Sun, Moon, and Ascendant (or sometimes the Ascendant ruler) in the natal chart.

The Part of Fortune falls in a specific house and zodiac sign in the natal chart, indicating areas of life where the individual may experience good fortune, opportunities, and fulfillment. It's often interpreted as a point of harmony and balance, where the individual can tap into their natural talents and strengths to achieve success and happiness.

 ## Location/Symbol

The part of fortune is typically represented by a circle with a cross in the centre.

CELESIAL POINTS

IMUM COELI

In astrology, Imum Coeli (The IC) represents points at the bottom of the natal chart, directly opposing the midheaven. It is also known as Nadir.

The IC represents one's roots, family background, home life, and the foundation of one's being. It's associated with the deepest, most private aspects of self, as well as one's emotional and psychological roots.

 ## Location/Symbol

The IC is located at the very bottom of the chart, opposite to the midheaven. It's situated on the cusp of the forth house, and is often symbolized by "IC" and a downward line.

CLOSING THOUGHTS

EMBRACING COSMIC WISDOM &. FULLFILLMENT

As we reach the end of this astrology book, may you find yourself equipped with newfound insights and understanding of the cosmic forces at play in your life. Remember, astrology is not just about predicting the future, but about understanding oneself, embracing opportunities for growth, and navigating life's journey with wisdom and intention. May the celestial wisdom shared in these pages guide you towards greater self-awareness, fulfillment, and connection to the universe. As you continue your exploration of the stars and planets, may you always trust in the magic of the cosmos and the infinite possibilities it holds. Wishing you cosmic blessings on your journey ahead...

Made in the USA
Middletown, DE
07 July 2024

56983819R00035